en • *courage* • ment

en • *courage* • ment

Ultimate Hope & Encouragement for Hard Times

Charles H. Spurgeon

R.P.B.
Northern

Published by R.P.B. Northern Publishing Company, United States of America

ISBN# 978-0-9981638-2-6

<u>Introduction</u>

Dear Reader, if you've got this book in your hands, chances are you're going through a rough time in your life or you know someone who is, and you're trying to figure out how to encourage that person—if so, please keep reading! Charles H. Spurgeon is widely regarded as one of the greatest pastors of the English language, yet he possessed a unique, down-to-earth ability to explain the Bible as if he were speaking directly *to you*, the reader, and nobody else. As you read these devotionals, forty in all, don't be surprised if you feel as though he's sitting right across from you, holding your hand, knowing and saying exactly what your heart needs to hear.

Of course, Pastor Spurgeon will not be the source of your encouragement—that comes only from God, and His revealed Word in the Bible—but Charles Spurgeon's words have an uncanny way of pointing us towards God's truths (which we seem so often to forget when things go wrong), and we trust that these devotionals will help you to look to God and find peace, strength, hope, and encouragement to get you or someone you care for through this tough time, whatever you, or they, are going through.

It's important to point out, from the outset, that the "encouragement" that God promises in His Word is only for Christians—that is, for people who have placed all their faith and trust in God's son, Jesus Christ, as their Lord and Savior, who took the punishment for our sins upon Himself on the cross, and then conquered death by rising from the grave, so that we may be forgiven, justified, and have eternal life, standing righteous before God in heaven someday. If you have *not trusted* in Jesus as your Savior, *please read the devotional for Day 1*, and place your faith in Him alone, before you do anything else—nothing is more important than this!

Charles Spurgeon left this earth long ago, having died on January 31, 1892, after many years of bad health. So, many of the subjects he wrote about in these devotionals, such as sickness and impending death, he was experiencing himself at the time of writing.

But unfortunately, the speech and writing of 1800's England is very difficult for most people who read or speak English to understand today. In fact, even many of the modern revisions and updates of Spurgeon's work are still inaccessible to people without a high level of expertise in the language. In other words, many young people—such as teenagers who face anxiety or depression, or people who haven't had the opportunity for lots of education—may find the writing out of touch, and would stop reading—yet these are often the very same people who need Pastor Spurgeon's encouragement the most! So this small portion of his devotional book, *Morning & Evening,* has been rewritten to be understandable and relatable to everyone, regardless of their background.

The Scriptures included in these devotionals are still in the King James Version of the Bible, because that's what Pastor Spurgeon himself would have been reading back then. But the editors have taken the liberty of updating the words that are commonly known to be archaic, and no longer used anymore. For example, every "thee" or "thou" in these verses are now translated as "you" in this volume. But for all intents and purposes, the meaning of the verse itself remains the same, and numerous other translations of the Bible have been consulted during the translation process to ensure accuracy.

Within the devotionals themselves, it's easy to see that Charles Spurgeon possessed such an all-encompassing knowledge of the Bible, because his writing is chock full of Biblical quotes (some are obvious, and some are more hidden) in addition to the main verse that starts off each devotional. In most of these cases, we have added a footnote that provides you with the actual verse reference that he's referring to—and you are highly encouraged to have a Bible handy at all times, and to consult it for these footnotes (as you should consult it for everything in your life). Reading the main verses and the footnote verses within the context of the surrounding verses in the Bible will increase your understanding of the Bible. And if you don't have a Bible, don't rest until you get one, for the very meaning and purpose of your life lies within its pages. And if all else fails, contact us at rpbnorthern@outlook.com, and we'll do our best to get one to you at little or no cost.

And finally, in a few spots, Pastor Spurgeon makes references to things or events from his time that probably wouldn't be easily understood by most readers today—in some of these places, the editors have done their best to slightly change the wording to bring the subject of conversation into the present day, and in other places they have added a short footnote, just to point you in the right direction as to what Pastor Spurgeon is referring to.

And with that, there's nothing else left to say, except "Happy reading!" Do your best to stick with it for all forty days, which is how long it rained while Noah was in the ark—and by the end of that tough, scary time, Noah probably had learned a lot about God, and His purpose in it all—the good times and the bad. And so just the same, we hope that these next forty days will make all the difference to you as you're going through your own personal struggle.

"Thank you, Lord, for giving us shepherds—pastors like Charles Spurgeon, who help point the way to You, and the truths in Your Word. Please use this book to encourage Your children, giving them hope when all seems lost."

-The Editors

Day 1

It is time to seek the Lord.
ঞ Hosea 10:12 ও

Dear Reader, if you have picked up this book, but are still unsaved, I pray that your heart will now be opened to receive the Lord. Maybe you are young—in the springtime of your life—and just like all of nature awakens in the spring, may every blossoming flower warn you that it is time to seek the Lord. Don't be out of tune with nature, but let your heart bud and bloom with holy desires.

"But," you might say, "I'm young and full of energy, and have no need of God right now in my life."

In response, I would beg you to give your youthful strength and energy to the Lord *now!* To me, it was an indescribable blessing in my life, that God called me when I was just a teenager—I could happily praise the Lord every day for it. It is true, salvation is priceless, no matter when it comes to a person, but oh!—an early salvation is worth twice as much! Young men and women, since you may die before you ever reach the prime of your life, "It is time to seek the Lord."

And you, who are starting to feel the first signs of decay, of getting older, you need to move all the faster: that raspy cough, that shortness of breath, or those circles under your eyes—these are all warnings that you should take seriously; for you it is definitely "time to seek the Lord." Do I see a little gray mixed in with your once luxurious curls?—years are creeping up on you quickly, and death is steadily, quickly marching nearer and nearer; may today's reading remind you to "set your house in order," making sure you are prepared for that day.

And finally, Dear Reader, if you are now advanced in life, let me beg you, let me *implore* you, not to delay any longer! By the grace of God, you still have today; and you should be thankful for that, but it is a limited time only, and it grows shorter with every tick of the clock. Here in this quiet room, on this first day of your reading this book, I speak to you as best I can through the type-written words on this page, and from my innermost soul, as God's servant, I'll put before you one last time this warning, "It is time to seek the Lord." Don't take this lightly—it may be your last call from destruction, God's final words of grace before it's too late.[1]

---

[1] Pastor Spurgeon is urging us to believe in the Gospel, which is the Good News of Jesus Christ. See Mark 1:14-15: "Now after John [the Baptist] was put in prison, Jesus came into Galilee, preaching the Gospel of the Kingdom of God, and saying, 'The time is fulfilled, and the Kingdom of God is at hand: repent [of your sins], and believe the Gospel.'" "What does it mean to believe in the Gospel?" you may ask? Romans 10:9 says "[t]hat if you will confess with your mouth the Lord Jesus, and believe in your heart that God has raised him from the dead, you will be saved." See also Acts 16:31, where the Philippian jailer asked Paul and Silas, "'What must I do to be saved?' And they said, 'Believe on the Lord Jesus Christ, and you will be saved, and your house.'"

Day 2

Casting all your worries upon Him;

because He cares for you.

ஒ 1 Peter 5:7 ௵

It is a wonderful way to take away your sorrow, when you can truly feel these words inside: "He cares for me." Dear Christian, do not dishonor your faith by always wearing a look of worry on your face—come, cast your burden upon your Lord. You are struggling beneath a weight that your Heavenly Father would not even feel—what feels like a crushing burden to you, would be to Him like no more than the smallest bit of dust weighed on the scale.

Oh, suffering child, please be patient—God, in His all-providing wisdom and care, has not forgotten about or passed you over. He is the One who feeds the sparrows,[1] and He will also give you what you need. Do not sit down and give up in despair—always be ever hopeful. Take hold of the weapons of faith[2] against a sea of trouble, and fight back (spiritually) against your worry, and God will help you overcome it.

---

[1] Matthew 10:29-31.
[2] The editors suggest prayer, and reading the Bible (the sword of the Spirit, Ephesians 6:17-18) as two of these "weapons."

There is One who cares for you. His eye is focused on you, His heart beats with pity for your sorrow, and his all-powerful hand will still bring you the help you need. The darkest cloud will be scattered in showers of mercy. The blackest gloom will turn into the light of morning. If you are one of His family, a Christian, He will bandage your wounds, and heal your broken heart. Don't let your troubles cause you to doubt His grace; instead, believe that He loves you as much in seasons of sadness as in times of happiness. What a peaceful and quiet life you might lead if you would leave the burden of providing to the God of providence! With a little oil in the jug, and a handful of flour in the jar, Elijah survived the famine,[3] and you will do the same. If God cares for you, why must you care even to the point of sadness, too? If you trust Him to save your soul, why would you not also trust Him to care for your body and life? He has never refused to carry your burdens; He has never fainted under their weight. So then, come along, my friend—be finished with anxious worry, and leave all your concerns behind, placing them in the hand of a gracious God.

Remember, nothing is so sweet as to

"Lie quietly in God's hands,
And know no will but His."

---

[3] 1 Kings 17:8-16.

Day 3

I will help you, says the Lord.

∞ Isaiah 41:14 ∞

Today let us hear the Lord Jesus speak to each one of us: "I will help you."

"It is just a small thing for Me, your God, to help you. Think about what I have done already. Do you really believe that I will not help you? I bought you with My blood. How could I not help you? ... I have died for you—the greatest thing of all—and if I've done that, wouldn't I do smaller things for you also? ... Help you? It's the least I could do for you—I have done more, and will do even more still. Before the world began I chose you. I made the covenant for you. I laid aside My glory and became a man for you; I gave up My life for you; and if I did all this, I will surely help you now. By helping you, I am giving you what I have bought for you already. If you needed a thousand times more help, I would give it to you; you are asking for just a little bit, compared with what I am ready to give. It is much for you to need, but it is nothing for me to give. ... Help you? Don't be afraid! If there were an ant at the door of your house asking for help, it would not ruin you to give him a handful of your food; and so also you are like just a tiny insect at the door of My unlimited wealth, my all-sufficiency. I will help you!"[1]

Oh my friend, isn't this enough? Do you need more strength than the omnipotence, the all-powerfulness, of the Trinity?[2] Do you want more wisdom than exists in the Father, more love than is shown in the Son, or more power than can be seen in the workings of the Holy Spirit? Bring here your empty pitcher! Surely this fountain will fill it. Hurry, gather up your desires, and bring them here—your emptiness, your sadness, your needs. Look!—this river of God is full for your supply; what could you possibly want besides this? Go forward then, my friend, with this as your strength. The Eternal God is your helper![3]

"Fear not, I am with thee; oh, be not dismayed!
I, I am your God, and will still give you aid."[4]

---

[1] See Romans 8:31-32.
[2] This is the Christian doctrine of God in three persons—the Father, the Son (Jesus Christ), and the Holy Spirit. See Matthew 28:19 for a reference to all three in a single verse.
[3] See also Deuteronomy 33:26, Psalm 33:20, and Psalm 115:9-11.
[4] Isaiah 41:10. See also Isaiah 43:1-3.

Day 4

He was very thirsty, and called on the Lord, and said, You have given this great deliverance into the hand of Your servant: and now will I die of thirst?

ॐ Judges 15:18 ☙

Samson was thirsty and ready to die. The difficulty was totally different from anything that the hero had ever encountered before. Now, think about it—simply quenching your thirst is nothing compared to being saved from a thousand Philistines! But when the thirst was upon him, Samson felt like that little difficulty he was going through in that moment was worse than the great difficulty that God had so specially rescued him from in the past. And so it is with us—it is very common for God's people, after they have enjoyed a great deliverance, to still find just a little bit of trouble to be too much for them. Samson kills a thousand Philistines, and piles them up in heaps, and then faints because he needs a little water! Jacob wrestles with God at Peniel, and managed to overcome his all-powerful opponent, and then goes "limping on his hip!"[5] How

---

[5] Genesis 32:22-31.

strange it is, that our strength seems to shrink right after we win the day—it's as if the Lord must teach us our littleness, our nothingness, in order to remind us of our boundaries. Samson was telling the truth when he bragged, "I have killed a thousand [of God's enemies]." But his prideful throat soon grew hoarse and raspy with thirst, causing him to humbly turn in prayer to God.

God has many ways of humbling His people. Dear child of God, if you've hit a very low point after previously receiving a great mercy from God, your situation is not at all unusual. When David had finally taken the throne of Israel, he said, "I am weak today, even though I've been anointed as king."[6] So also, you should expect to feel weakest when you are enjoying your greatest triumph. If God has brought about great deliverances for you in the past, your present difficulty is only like Samson's thirst, and the Lord will not let you faint, nor will He allow the "Philistines" in your life to triumph over you. The road of sorrow is the road to heaven, but there are wells of refreshing water all along the route. So, you Brothers and Sisters going through trials, cheer your hearts with Samson's words, and rest assured that God will deliver you before too long.

---

[6] 2 Samuel 3:39.

Day 5

Does Job fear God for nothing?

❧ Job 1:9 ☙

This was the wicked question that Satan asked about that righteous man from so long ago, but there are many people today that this question could also be asked about—and rightly so, because they appear to love God in certain ways because He gives them prosperity; but if things went wrong, as they did for Job, these people would give up their show of faith in God. If they see that their lives have moved along comfortably since the time that they supposedly became Christians, then they will continue to love God in their poor, worldly way; but the moment they have to endure real hardship and adversity, they will rebel against the Lord. Their love is the love of the food on the table, not of the host who provides it; a love given to the plentiful refrigerator or kitchen pantry, not to the master of the house who fills it. As for the true Christian, he or she expects to have their reward in the next life, and to endure hardness in this world. The promise of the old covenant was prosperity, but the promise of the new covenant is adversity.[1] Remember Christ's words—"Every branch in me that does not bear fruit he takes away, and every branch that bears fruit, he prunes, that it may produce more fruit."[2] So, if you produce fruit, you will have to endure hardship.

"Oh no!" you might say, "That is a terrible outlook!"

But these hardships work out such precious results, that Christians who are going through them must learn to rejoice in these troubles, because as their troubles increase, so also are their comforts and consolations increased by Christ Jesus. Rest assured, if you are a child of God, you will be no stranger to discipline. Sooner or later every bar of gold must pass through the fire.[3] Do not be afraid, but instead rejoice and be happy that such fruitful times are in store for you, because in them you will be weaned from earth and made ready for heaven; you will be changed—saved from an attitude that clings to the things of earth today, and you'll be made to desire those eternal things which are so soon to be revealed to you. In other words, if you may have felt at some point, even today, that you have been serving God for nothing, such difficulties will bring you to rejoicing in the infinite reward of the future.

---

[1] In the Old Testament, God promised Israel that they would be prosperous if they obeyed His law. For example, see Deuteronomy 28. But on the other hand, Jesus never promised prosperity in this life if we follow Him (see Matthew 16:24-26).

[2] John 15:2.

[3] This is a reference to the method of refining gold by heating it with fire.

Day 6

Surely he will deliver you

from the snare of the fowler.

ଛ Psalm 91:3 ଓ

God delivers, or saves, His people from the snare of the fowler[1] in two ways. The first way: "from." And the second way: "out of."

First, He delivers them *from* the snare—He does not let them get caught in it at all; or secondly, if they should happen to get caught in it, He delivers them *out of* it. The first promise is the most precious to some; the second is the best to others. "He will deliver you from the snare." How? Trouble is often the means, or the way, that God uses to deliver us—God knows that our backsliding and our laziness in spiritual things will soon end in our destruction, and so He mercifully sends the rod (in other words, the rod of discipline[2]). We may say, "Lord, why is this?" not knowing that our trouble has been the means of keeping us out of far greater evil. In this way, many have been saved from ruin by their own sorrows and

---

[1] A fowler is someone who hunts or traps wild birds for food.
[2] Proverbs 13:24.

the heavy crosses they've had to bear[3]—in this way, the Father's discipline has frightened the birds from the danger of the net, trap, or snare. At other times, God keeps His people from the snare of the fowler by giving them great spiritual strength, so that when they are tempted to do evil they say, "How can I do this great wickedness, and sin against God?"[4]

But what a blessing to know that even if a believer, in a moment of weakness, gives in to temptation and becomes caught in the net, yet even then God will bring him or her out of it! Dear backslider—you may be cast down, at a low point in your life, but do not despair. Even though you have been a wanderer, hear what your Redeemer says: "Return, O backsliding children; I will have mercy upon you."[5] But you may say that you can't return, because you are a prisoner now. But then listen again to the promise: "Surely He will deliver you out of the snare of the fowler." You will even still be brought out of all the evil that you've fallen into, and though you will never stop feeling sorrow over your sinful ways, even so He that has loved you will not send you away; He will receive you, and give you joy and gladness, so that the bones which He has broken may rejoice.[6] You can be sure, no "bird of paradise" will die in the fowler's net.

---

[3] Matthew 10:38.
[4] Genesis 39:9.
[5] See, for example, Jeremiah 3:12-22.
[6] Psalm 51:8.

Day 7

I will mention the lovingkindnesses of the Lord, and the praises of the Lord, according to all that the Lord has given to us.

∞ Isaiah 63:7 ∞

Can't you do this? Aren't there any mercies which you have experienced? Even though things seem gloomy now, are you really able to forget that blessed hour when Jesus met you, and said, "Come unto me"?[1] Can't you remember that completely joyful moment when He broke your shackles, and smashed your chains to pieces, and said, "I came to break your bonds and set you free"?[2]

Or, if that first love experienced at your salvation has somehow been forgotten, then still there must surely be some precious milestone along the road of life, not quite grown over with moss, where you can find a happy memory of His mercy towards you? What, did you never have a sickness like that you're suffering now, and did He not heal you? Were you never poor before, and did He not supply your needs? Were you never in desperation before, and did He not get you out

---

[1] Matthew 11:28-30.
[2] See, for example, John 8:36, and John 10:10.

23

of trouble?—So get up, and go to the river of your experience, and pull up a few reeds from those memories, and weave them into a basket, in which your childlike faith may float safely on the stream.[3] *Do not forget* what your God has done for you; turn back through the pages of your book of memories, and think about those days from long ago in your life. Can't you remember the hill at Mizar? Didn't the Lord meet with you at Mount Hermon?[4] Have you never climbed the Delectable Mountains?[5] Have you never been helped in time of need? To the contrary—I know that you have. Go back, then, a little way to the precious mercies of yesterday; and even though everything may be dark now, light up the lamps of the past, and they will glitter through the darkness, and you will trust in the Lord till the day breaks and the shadows flee away. "Remember, O LORD, your tender mercies and your loving-kindnesses, for they have been [with us from long ago]."[6]

---

[3] This analogy is based on the baby Moses being placed in a basket on the River Nile. See Exodus 2:3.

[4] See Psalm 42:6. The Psalmist's meaning is uncertain. It may mean that the psalmist will remember to praise God anywhere, from both lowly (Mizar) and grand (Hermon) places. Or, as Pastor Spurgeon seems to imply, this is a reference to a happy place and time in Israel's history, which the psalmist is remembering in order to bring him out of his depression.

[5] This is a reference to the book, *Pilgrim's Progress*. The Delectable Mountains were a place where the "Pilgrim," Christian, was able "to behold the gardens and orchards, the vineyards and fountains of water; where also they drank and washed themselves, and did freely eat of the vineyards"—clearly, it was a time of God's provision in his life.

[6] Psalm 25:6. See also Psalm 103:4-5.

Day 8

The love of the Lord.

ɞɔ Hosea 3:1 03

Dear Believer, look back through all your experience, and think of the way in which the Lord your God has led you in the wilderness, and how He has fed and clothed you every day—how He has tolerated all of your ingratitude—how He has put up with all of your complaints, and all of your longings after the meat of Egypt—how He has opened the rock to supply you, and fed you with manna that came down from heaven.[1] Think of how His grace has been sufficient for you in all your troubles—how His blood has been a pardon to you for all your sins—how His rod and His staff have comforted you.[2] Then, after you've looked back upon the love of the Lord, next let faith look forward to His love in the future—don't forget that Christ's covenant and blood have something more in them than just the past. He who has loved you and pardoned you up to this point, will never cease to love and

---

[1] See Exodus 16:3 and 17:5-7. These are all references to the Israelites' grumbling in the desert—despite God's gracious deliverance from slavery in Egypt, and provision for them up to that point. They said that they would rather return to Egypt and eat well as slaves, than continue hungry any longer in the desert while on their way to the Promised Land.
[2] Psalm 23:4.

pardon you. He is Alpha, and He will be Omega also: He is first, and He will be last.[3] Therefore, think to yourself, whenever you pass through the valley of the shadow of death, you have no reason to fear evil, for He is with you.[4] Whenever you find yourself standing in the cold waters of Jordan,[5] you don't need to be afraid, because death cannot separate you from His love; and whenever you enter into the mysteries of eternity you won't tremble in fear, "For I am persuaded, that neither death; nor life, nor angels [or demons], nor principalities [governments and rulers], nor powers, nor things present, nor things future, nor height, nor depth, nor any other creature, will be able to separate us from the love of God, which is in Christ Jesus our Lord."[6]

Now, Believer, isn't your soul's love refreshed? Doesn't this make you love Jesus? If you soar through the unlimited vastness of this love, doesn't this fuel your heart and encourage you all the more to find your joy in the Lord your God? Surely as we meditate on "the love of the Lord," our hearts burn within us,[7] and we long to love Him more.

---

[3] See Revelation 1:8. Alpha is the first letter, and Omega is the last letter of the Greek alphabet.
[4] Psalm 23:4.
[5] The Jordan River has traditionally been used as a metaphor for death—just as the Israelites crossed the Jordan River to enter the Promised Land, so also Christians must pass through death before arriving at their "Promised Land."
[6] Romans 8:38-39. The words in brackets have been included in numerous other translations of this verse.
[7] See, for example, Luke 24:32.

Day 9

For as the sufferings of Christ abound in us,

so our consolation also abounds by Christ.

ஐ 2 Corinthians 1:5 ଔ

There is a blessed proportion—God, the Ruler of Providence, holds a pair of scales—in the one side He puts His people's trials, and in the other He puts their consolations. When the scale of trial is nearly empty, you will always find the scale of consolation in nearly the same condition; and when the scale of trials is full, you will find the scale of consolation just as heavy. When the black clouds gather the most, the light is the more brightly revealed to us. When the darkness of night lowers, and the storm is coming on, the Heavenly Captain is always closest to His crew. It is a wonderful thing to remember, that when we are most cast down, then it is that we are most lifted up by the comforts and consolations of the Spirit. One reason is, because trials make more room for consolation—great hearts can only be made by great troubles. Trouble in a person's life is like a shovel, which digs the reservoir of comfort deeper, and makes more room for consolation. God comes into our heart—He finds it full—He begins to break our comforts and to make it empty; then there is more room for grace. The humbler a man lies, the more comfort he will always have, because he will be more ready to receive it.

Another reason why we are often most happy in our troubles, is this—during troubles, we have the closest contact with God. When the barn is full, people can live without God; or, when the purse or wallet is bursting with gold, we try to get by without praying so much. But once our creature comforts are taken away, then we want our God; once the house is cleansed of idols, then we are compelled to honor Jehovah. "Out of the depths have I cried unto you, O LORD."[1] There is no cry so good, so relieving, as that which comes from the deep valley between mountains; no prayer half so strong as that which comes up from the depths of the soul, through deep trials and afflictions. And so, they bring us to God, and we are happier for it; because nearness to God *is happiness*. Come on, troubled Believer—do not worry over your heavy troubles, for they bring news of even greater mercies soon to come.

---

[1] Psalm 130:1.

Day 10

Behold, what manner of love the Father has given to us, that we should be called the sons of God: therefore the world doesn't know us, because it didn't know Him. Beloved, now we are the sons of God . . .

෨ 1 John 3:1, 2 ෪

"Behold, what manner of love the Father has given to us." Think about who we were, and what we still feel ourselves to be, even now, when corruption is powerful in us—think about this, and you will be amazed at our adoption. We are called "the sons of God." What an important relationship is that of a son or daughter, and what privileges it brings! What care and tenderness they expect from their father, and what love the father feels towards them! But all that, and more than that, we now have through Christ. As for the temporary drawback of suffering with Jesus, this we accept as an honor: "Therefore the world doesn't know us, because it didn't know Him." We are content, happy, to be unknown with Him in His humiliation, because someday we will be exalted and honored with Him. "Beloved, now we are the sons of God." That is easy to read, but it is not so easy to *feel*. How are things with your heart today? Are you in the lowest depths of sorrow? Does corruption, or sinful desire, rise within your spirit, and grace seems like a little, poor spark trampled down underfoot? Does your faith almost fail you? If so, then don't be afraid—you're not supposed to base your life on how good you feel, or how great you perform day-to-day as a Christian; instead, you *must* live simply by faith in Christ. With all these things against us *now*, in the very depths of our sorrow, wherever we may be *now*, as much in the valley as on the mountain: "Beloved, *now* we are the sons of God."

"Ah, but," you say, "look at how poorly I am clothed!—my Christian life doesn't seem bright; my righteousness doesn't shine with any glory that I can see." But then read the next: "It does not yet appear what we will be; but we know that, when He [Jesus Christ] will appear, we will be like Him." The Holy Spirit will purify our minds, and divine power will make our bodies perfect, and then "we will see Him as He is."[1]

---

[1] 1 John 3:2.

Day 11

And his allowance was a continual allowance given to him by the king, a daily ration for every day, all the days of his life.

☙ 2 Kings 25:30 ❧

Jehoiachin was not sent away from the king's palace with a stockpile to last him for months, but rather his provision was given to him in the form of a daily pension. In this situation, we can easily picture the happy position of all the Lord's people. A daily portion is all that a person really wants. We do not need tomorrow's supplies; that day has not yet dawned, and the things that we might want then haven't even been born yet—the thirst that we may suffer in the month of June does not need to be quenched in February, for we do not feel it yet. Instead, if we have enough for each day as the days arrive, then we will never know what it feels like to want for things. Sufficient for the day is all that we can enjoy. We cannot eat or drink or wear more than the day's supply of food and clothing; and to have extra will give us the burden of storing it, and the anxiety of protecting it against thieves. One walking stick helps a traveler, but a bundle of them becomes a heavy burden. "Enough" is not only as good as a feast, but it is all that even a glutton can truly enjoy. Enough for the day—this is all that we should expect; a craving for more than this is ungrateful. When our Father does not give us more, we should be content with his daily allowance. Jehoiachin's case is ours—we have a sure portion, a portion given to us by the king, a gracious portion, and a perpetual portion. This is surely a good reason for thankfulness.

Beloved Christian Reader, in matters of grace you also need a daily supply. You have no store or stockpile of strength. Day by day you must seek help from above, from God. It is a very sweet assurance that a daily portion is provided for you. In the Word, through the ministry, by meditation, in prayer, and waiting upon God you will receive renewed strength. In Jesus, everything that you need has been laid up, set aside for you as your daily portion, and you may always enjoy your continual allowance. *Never go hungry while the daily bread of grace is on the table of mercy.*[1]

---

[1] See also Matthew 6:11 and Luke 11:3.

Day 12

I have learned, in whatever state I am ...

to be content.

∞ Philippians 4:11 ∞

These words show us that contentment is not the natural state of mankind. As the old proverb goes, "Ill weeds grow apace"[1]—envy, discontentment, and grumbling are as natural to men and women as thorns are to the soil. In nature, we don't need to sow seeds for thistles and brambles; they come up naturally enough, because they are indigenous to earth. And so, we never need to teach people how to complain— they complain fast enough without any education. But the precious things of the earth must be cultivated—if we want to have wheat, we must plough and sow; if we want flowers, there must be the garden, and all the careful labor of the gardener. Now, contentment is one of the flowers of heaven, and if we would have it, it must be cultivated; it will not grow in us by nature; it is the new nature in Christ alone that can

---

[1] "Apace" is an archaic word meaning "quickly."

produce it, and even then we must be especially careful and watchful that we maintain and cultivate the grace which God has sown in us. Paul says, "I have *learned* . . . to be content;" this basically implies that even the great Apostle Paul did not know how at one time—it required pain and effort on his part to understand the mystery of that great truth. No doubt he sometimes thought he had finally learned how to be content, and then broke down again. And then, when at last he had finally gained this insight, and could say, "In whatever state I am in, I have learned to be content," he was an old, gray-headed man, on the edge of the grave—a poor prisoner shut up in Nero's dungeon at Rome.[2] And we, too, should be willing to endure Paul's misery, and to share the cold dungeon with him, if this discipline might in any way help us to achieve even the slightest degree of his contentment. But don't let yourself think that you can become contented through learning alone, or that you can learn any measure of contentment without discipline first. It is not a power that may be exercised naturally, but a grace to be acquired gradually. We know this from experience. My Brother or Sister, hush that complaining, natural though it may be, and continue as a hardworking student in the College of Contentment.

---

[2] Paul actually wrote Philippians while a prisoner in Rome, around 60 – 62 A.D. He was briefly released, then re-imprisoned, and finally executed for his faith in Christ, sometime around 66 – 67 A.D.

Day 13

Although the LORD was there.

荣 Ezekiel 35:10 荢

The Princes of Edom saw that the whole country of Israel looked desolate, deserted, and they expected it to be an easy conquest; but there was one great difficulty in their way—quite unknown to them—"The LORD was there"; and in His presence lay the special security of the chosen land. And it's the same today: however the enemies of God's people might plot or scheme, there is still the same powerful barrier to ruin their evil plans. The saints[1] are God's heritage, and He is with them, in the midst of them, and will protect His own. What comfort this promise provides to us in our troubles and spiritual conflicts! We are constantly opposed, and yet we are perpetually preserved! How often Satan shoots his arrows against our faith, but our faith defies the power of his fiery darts; they are not only deflected, but they are quenched upon our "shield of faith,[2] for "the LORD is there." Our good

---

[1] The term "saint" is used in the Bible to speak of any true Christian, rather than a special "upper-class" of Christians. See, e.g., 1 Corinthians 1:2, or Romans 1:6-7. If you are truly saved, Pastor Spurgeon is speaking to you.
[2] See Ephesians 6:16.

works are the subjects of Satan's attacks. There has never been a saint yet with a good virtue or quality from God, that was not the target of hellish bullets—whether it be bright and sparkling hope, or warm and fervent love, or all-enduring patience, or enthusiasm flaming like coals of fire—whatever that virtue may be, the old enemy of everything that is good (the devil) has tried to destroy it. The only reason why anything virtuous or lovely survives at all in us is this: "the LORD is there."

If the Lord is with us all through this life, then just the same we can have confidence and need not fear death; because when we are getting close to death, we will find that "the LORD is there." Where the crashing waves are most violent, and the water is most chilling, we will still feel the bottom, and know that it is good—our feet will stand upon the Rock of Ages when time is passing away. Beloved, from the first day of a Christian's life to the last, the only reason why he or she does not perish is because "the LORD is there." So, if the God of everlasting love should ever happen to change, and leave His chosen people to perish, then the Church of God would be destroyed; *but we know this will never happen, because it is written*, JEHOVAH SHAMMAH, "The LORD is there."

Day 14

Show me why you contend with me.

ဢ Job 10:2 ဢ

Oh Weary Soul, maybe the Lord is doing this to develop your graces—your Christian virtue and character. Some of these graces would never be discovered if it were not for your trials. Don't you know that your faith never looks as magnificent in beautiful summer weather as it does in the hardness of winter? Love is too often like a glow-worm, showing just a tiny bit of light, and it cannot be seen unless it is in the midst of surrounding darkness. Hope itself is like a star—unable to be seen in the sunshine of prosperity, and only to be discovered in the night of adversity. Afflictions and hardships are often the black backgrounds in which God sets the jewels of His children's graces, to make them shine all the better. It was just a little while ago that you were on your knees, praying, "Lord, I fear I have no faith: let me know that I have faith." Wasn't this really (although perhaps unconsciously), praying for trials?—because how can you know that you have faith until your faith is exercised, or tested? You can depend upon it—

God often sends us trials so that our Christian character may be discovered, and that we may be assured of its existence. And even more, we're not just talking about mere discovery— real growth in grace is the result of these sacred trials. God often takes away our comforts and our privileges in order to make us better Christians. He trains His soldiers, not in tents of easiness and luxury, but by sending them out and getting them used to forced marches and hard service. He makes them cross through streams, and swim through rivers, and climb mountains, and walk many long miles with heavy packs of sorrow on their backs. Well, Dear Christian, could this be the reason for the troubles you're passing through right now? Can it be that maybe the Lord is bringing out your graces, your Christian virtues, like faith, hope, and love, and making them grow? Isn't this the reason why He is contending with you?

"Trials make the promise sweet;
Trials give new life to prayer;
Trials bring me to His feet,
Lay me low, and keep me there."

Day 15

God, who comforts those that are cast down.

⯍ 2 Corinthians 7:6 ⯎

And who comforts like Him? Go to some poor, melancholy, distressed child of God; tell him sweet promises, and whisper in his ear some special words of comfort; but he is like the deaf snake—he doesn't listen to the voice of the snake charmer, no matter how wisely the charmer plays his tune. He is drinking gall and wormwood,[1] and no matter how hard you try to comfort him, you'll only get a note or two of mournful resignation from that person; you won't get him or her to sing any psalms of praise, no hallelujahs, no joyful sonnets. But let God come to His child, let Him lift up that downcast heart, and the mourner's eyes will glisten with hope. Can't you just hear that same person now singing?:

> *"Tis paradise, if you are here;*
> *If you depart, 'tis hell"*

Try as you might, you could not have cheered up that poor soul, but the Lord has done it; "He is the God of all comfort."[2]

---

[1] Gall and wormwood are bitter spices mentioned several places in the Bible. See, for example, Lamentations 3:15, 19.

[2] 2 Corinthians 1:3.

There is no balm in Gilead,[3] but there is healing balm in God. There is no physician among the *creatures*, but the *Creator* is Jehovah-rophi (the LORD who heals you).[4] It is marvelous how one sweet word of God will make whole songs for Christians. One word of God is like a piece of gold, and the Christian is the gold-worker, who can hammer that promise out for whole weeks.

So, then, poor Christian, you don't need to sit down in despair. Go to the Comforter, and ask Him to give you consolation. Think of yourself as a poor, dry well—it's been said that when a pump runs dry, to fix it you must first of all pour water down it, and then you will get more water from the well. So, Christian, when you are dry, go to God, ask Him to spread His joy throughout your heart, and then your joy will be full. Do not go to earthly friends for comfort, for you will find them to be like Job's comforters in the end[5]; instead, go first and foremost to your "God, who comforts those that are cast down,"[6] and you will soon say, "In the multitude of my [anxious] thoughts within me, your comforts delight my soul."[7]

---

3 See Jeremiah 8:22. A balm is a healing cream applied directly to the skin. Gilead was known for its medicine.

4 Exodus 15:22-26.

5 See the book of Job. During Job's severe trials, his friends attempted to comfort and advise him; but in the end their advice proved to be wrong, and only God was able to provide the answers to Job's questions.

6 2 Corinthians 7:6.

7 Psalm 94:19.

Day 16

I will never leave you.

ᔓ Hebrews 13:5 **ᔓ**

No promise needs to be interpreted privately—whatever God has said to any one believer, He has said to all of them. When He opens a well for one, it is so that all may drink. When He opens a granary or warehouse door to give out food, it may have been for just one starving man at that moment, but all hungry Christians may come and feed too. Dear Believer, whether God gave the word to Abraham or to Moses, it does not matter—He has given it to you also as a child of the same covenant. None of God's highest blessings are too tall for you, nor is his wide mercy too far-reaching for you. Lift up your eyes to the north and to the south, to the east and to the west, for all this is yours. Climb to the top of Mount Pisgah, and view the utmost limit of the divine promise, for the land is all yours. There is not a brook of living water of which you may not drink. If the land flows with milk and honey, eat the honey and drink the milk, because both are yours.[1]

---

[1] See Deuteronomy 3:27, 34:1-4. These are references to Moses' viewing of the bounty and goodness of the Promised Land from the top of Mount Pisgah.

Christian, believe *boldly*, because He has said, "I will never leave you, nor forsake you." In this promise, God gives to His people everything: "I will never leave you." In this case, no part of God's character can ever stop working for us. Is He mighty?—He will show Himself strong on behalf of those who trust Him. Is He love?—then with lovingkindness He will have mercy upon us. Whatever good and perfect attributes or qualities make up God's character, every one of them to its fullest extent will be working on our side. To sum it all up—there is nothing you can want, there is nothing you can ask for, there is nothing you can need in time or in eternity, there is nothing living, nothing dying, there is nothing in this world, nothing in the next world, there is nothing now, nothing at the resurrection-morning, nothing in heaven which is not contained in this text—"I will never leave you, nor forsake you."

Day 17

Take up the cross, and follow Me.

ᔕ Luke 9:23 ભ

You do not have the ability to make your own cross (although unbelief is a master carpenter at cross-making); neither are you allowed to choose your own cross (although your own self-will would gladly do so). Rather, your cross is prepared and appointed for you by divine love, and you must cheerfully accept it; you must take up the cross as your chosen badge and burden, and should not stand grumbling or complaining at it. This very day Jesus is calling you to submit your shoulder to His easy yoke.[1] Do not kick at it like a spoiled child, or trample on it in self-pride, or fall under it in despair, or run away from it in fear, but take it up like a true follower of Jesus. Jesus was a cross-bearer; He leads the way in the path of sorrow. Surely you could not ask for a better guide! And if He carried a cross, what nobler burden could you possibly desire? The *Via Crucis*[2] is the way of safety—don't be afraid to tread upon its thorny paths!

---

[1] Matthew 11:30.
[2] Latin for "The Way of the Cross."

Beloved, the cross is not made of light feathers, or lined with soft velvet—it is heavy and unpleasant to disobedient shoulders. But it is not an iron cross (although your fears may have painted it with iron colors); it is a wooden cross, and a man or woman can carry it, for the Man of Sorrows has already tested the load for you. Take up your cross, and by the power of the Spirit of God you will soon be so in love with it, that just like Moses, you would not trade your sufferings for Christ for all the treasures of Egypt.[3] If you remember that Jesus carried it, it will be a lovely thing to you. If you remember that the reward of a crown will soon follow, then that thought of coming glory will greatly lighten the present heaviness of trouble.

May the Lord help you to bow your spirit in submission to His divine will before you go to sleep this very night, so that waking with tomorrow's sun, you'll approach the day's cross with the holy and submissive attitude of a true follower of the Crucified.

---

[3] Hebrews 11:26.

Day 18

I will cause the shower to come down in its season; there will be showers of blessing.

🔊 Ezekiel 34:26 ✂

Here is sovereign mercy—"I will give them the shower in its season." Isn't this sovereign, divine mercy?—for who can say, "I will give them showers," except for God? There is only one voice that can speak to the clouds, and tell them to bring the rain. Who sends down the rain upon the earth? Who scatters the showers upon the green trees and grass? Isn't it the Lord who does these things? So also grace is the gift of God, and is not to be created by man.

It is also *needed* grace. What would the ground do without showers? You may break up the clods of dirt, you may sow your seeds, but what can you do without the rain? And just as desperately needed is the divine blessing. You labor in vain until God gives those much-needed showers, and sends salvation down. And of course, it is *abundant* grace: "I will send them showers." It does not say, "I will send them raindrops," but rather it says "showers." So it is the same way with grace. If God gives a blessing, He usually gives it in such a measure that there isn't even enough room to receive it. Overflowing grace! Ah, yes!—we want overflowing grace to keep us humble, to make us prayerful, to make us holy; overflowing grace to make us zealous, to preserve us through this life, and at last to land us in heaven. We cannot live the Christian life without saturating showers of grace.

Again, it is *seasonable* grace. "I will cause the shower to come down in its season." What is your season this day? Is it the season of drought? Then that is the season for showers. Is it a season of great heaviness and black clouds? Then that is the season for showers. "As your days, so will your strength be."[1] And here is a varied blessing. "I will give you *showers* of blessing." The word is in the plural. All kinds of blessings God will send. All God's blessings go together, like links in a golden chain. If He gives grace for conversion to the Christian life, He will also give grace for comforting—He will send "showers of blessing." If you are feeling like a dry, parched, thirsty plant, then look up today, and open your leaves and flowers (your *heart* and *soul*) for a heavenly watering!

---

[1] Deuteronomy 33:25.

Day 19

O Lord of hosts, how long will you not have mercy upon Jerusalem? . . . And the Lord answered the angel . . . with good words and comfortable words.

so Zechariah 1:12, 13 cs

What a sweet answer to an anxious question! Let us rejoice in it today. Oh Zion,[1] there are good things in store for you; your time of toiling and trouble will soon be over; your children will be delivered; your captivity will end. Patiently endure the rod of discipline for a season, and under the darkness still trust in God, because His love burns toward you. God loves the church with a love too deep for human imagination: He loves her with all His infinite heart. Therefore, let her children be of good courage; no one can be far from prosperity when God speaks to them "with good words and comfortable words." The prophet Zechariah goes on to tell us what these

---

[1] The word "Zion" is used in various places in the Bible to refer to a literal area in or around Jerusalem; in other places it is used figuratively to refer to God's Kingdom, and also to Heaven.

47

comfortable words are: "I am jealous for Jerusalem and for Zion with a great jealousy."[2] The Lord loves His church so much that He cannot bear for her to go astray to others; and even then, when she has gone astray, He cannot bear that she should suffer too much or too heavily. He will not have his enemies hurt her: He is displeased with them because they increase her misery. When God seems most to leave His church, His heart is still warm towards her. History shows that whenever God uses a rod to discipline His servants, He always breaks it afterward, as if He hated the rod which gave his children pain. "Like a father pities his children, so the Lord pities them that fear Him."[3] God has not forgotten us because He disciplines us—the strikes from His rod do not in any way evidence or show that He is lacking in love. If this is true of His church collectively, as a whole, then it logically must apply to each individual member. You may fear that the Lord has passed you by, but this is not true: He who counts the stars, and calls them by their names,[4] is in no danger of forgetting His own children. He knows your case as thoroughly as if you were the only creature He ever made, or the only saint He ever loved. Approach Him and be at peace.

---

2 Zechariah 1:14.
3 Psalm 103:13.
4 Psalm 147:4.

Day 20

You have made the Lord, the Most High who is my refuge, your dwelling place.

ஐ Psalm 91:9 ௲

The Israelites in the wilderness were continually exposed to change. Whenever the pillar of cloud and fire stopped moving, then the tents were pitched; but tomorrow, before the morning sun had risen, the trumpet sounded, the Ark of the Covenant was in motion, and the fiery, cloudy pillar was leading the way through the narrow passageways of the mountains, up the hillsides, or along the dry wastelands of the wilderness.[1] They barely had any time to rest a little before they heard the sound of "Away!—this is not your rest; you must still be journeying onward towards Canaan!" They never stayed long in one place. Even the refreshment of the water wells and palm trees could not detain them. But they had a constant home in their God; His cloudy pillar was the roof over their heads during the day, and its flame was like their

---

[1] See, for example, Exodus 13:21-22.

household fireplace by night.

They always had to go onward from place to place, continually changing, never having time to settle, and to say, "Now we are secure; in this place we will dwell."

"But," Moses seems to say, "even though we are always changing, Lord, you have been our dwelling-place, our home, throughout all generations."[2] The Christian never sees, never knows, any change with regard to God. He or she may be rich today and poor tomorrow; they may be sick today and in good health tomorrow, or in happiness today, but distressed tomorrow—but there is no change with regard to his or her relationship to God. If He loved me yesterday, He loves me today. My blessed Lord is like my unmovable mansion of rest—let my earthly plans be ruined; let my hopes be destroyed; let joy be withered; let mold and mildew destroy everything—no matter what, I have lost nothing of what I have in God. He is "my strong dwelling place that I can continually resort to for safety."[3] I am a drifting pilgrim in this world,[4] but I am always at home in my God. In the earth I wander, but in God I live in a place of quiet strength and safety.

---

[2] See, for example, Psalm 90:1.
[3] Psalm 71:3.
[4] See Hebrews 11: 13 for a comparison of the Christian life to that of a pilgrim, or stranger in this world.

Day 21

The barrel of flour did not go empty, neither did the jar of oil run out, according to the word of the Lord, which He spoke by Elijah.

☙ 1 Kings 17:16 ❧

See the faithfulness of divine love. Notice that this woman had daily necessities—she had herself and her son to feed in a time of famine; and now, in addition, the prophet Elijah needed to be fed, too. But even though the need was triple, yet the supply of food was never used up because she had a constant supply. Each day she went to the barrel to get more flour, but yet each day it remained the same.

You, Dear Reader, also have daily necessities, and because they come so frequently, you tend to fear that the barrel of flour will one day be empty, and the jar of oil will fail you. But rest assured that, according to the Word of God, this will not happen. Each day, even though it brings plenty of trouble with it, will also bring enough help. Even if you miraculously lived to be older than Methuselah,[1] and even if

---

[1] According to Genesis 5:27, Methuselah lived to be 969 years old.

your needs were as many as the sands of the seashore, yet even then would God's grace and mercy last through all your necessities—and you will never know what it's like to really lack.

For three long years, in this widow's days, there was never a cloud in the sky during the day, and underneath the starry sky at night not even a single drop of dew touched the wicked earth. Famine, and desolation, and death, turned the land into a howling wasteland, but this woman was never hungry. Instead, she was always joyful in abundance. So will it be with you—you will see the sinner's hope disappear, for they trust in their own internal strength; you will see the proud Pharisee's[2] confidence collapse, for he builds his hope upon the unstable, shifting sand.[3] You will see even your own plans blasted and withered, but you yourself will find that your place of defense will be within the fortress of solid rock: "Your bread will be given you, and your water will be sure."[4] Better to have God for your guardian, than to have all the money in the world in your possession. You may be able to spend all the wealth of the world, but the infinite riches of God you'll never be able to use up.

---

[2] The Pharisees were the religious leaders in Israel during the time of Christ; the Gospels often characterize them as prideful and hypocritical. See, for example Matthew 23:1-36.
[3] Matthew 7:26.
[4] Isaiah 33:16

Day 22

I have chosen you in the furnace of affliction.

🜚 Isaiah 48:10 🜚

Dear Believers who are experiencing trouble right now, comfort yourself with this thought: God says, "I have chosen you in the furnace of affliction." Doesn't this message come like a soft shower, quenching the fury of the flame? Yes! It's like fireproof armor, against which the heat has no power. Let troubles and afflictions come—God has chosen me. *Poverty*, you may walk right in at my door, but God is in the house already, and He has chosen me. *Sickness*, you may intrude, but I have medicine ready—God has chosen me. Whatever happens to me in this valley of tears, I know that He has "chosen" me.

If, Dear Believer, you require even greater comfort, remember that you have the Son of Man with you in the furnace.[1] In that silent room of yours, there is sitting by your side One whom you have not seen, but whom you love[2]; and oftentimes when you are not even aware, He lovingly makes

---

[1] Daniel 3:23-25.
[2] 1 Peter 1:6-9. See also John 20:29.

your bed in your affliction, and smooths your pillow for you. You are in poverty; but in that lovely house of yours the Lord of life and glory is a frequent visitor. He loves to come into these lonely, desolate places in order to visit you. Your friend sticks closely to you. You cannot see Him, but you might feel the pressure of His hands. Don't you hear His voice?—Even in the valley of the shadow of death, He says, "Don't be afraid, for I am with you; don't be discouraged, for I am your God."[3]

Remember those encouraging words of Julius Caesar: "Fear not—you carry Caesar and all his fortune."[4] And in a far greater way, Christian, *don't be afraid*—Jesus is with you! In all your fiery trials, His presence is both your comfort and safety. He will never leave anyone whom He has chosen for His own. "Don't be afraid, for I am with you," is His certain message of promise to His chosen ones in the "furnace of affliction." Won't you then, hold on tightly to Christ, and say—

"Through floods and flames, if Jesus leads,
I'll follow where He goes."

---

[3] Isaiah 41:10. See also Psalm 23:4.
[4] These words were said to the captain of the ship that was carrying Julius Caesar during a bad storm at sea, meant to encourage the captain to press onward boldly, knowing that Caesar—his king—was with him.

Day 23

My grace is sufficient for you.

ᔥ 2 Corinthians 12:9 ᔥ

If none of God's servants were poor and troubled—if all Christians were rich and had easy lives—we would never know half as much about the comfort and consolation of God's divine grace. When we see the homeless person who has nowhere to lay his head, but who can still say, "I'll trust in God," or when we see the poor person starving on bread and water, who still gives glory to Jesus; when we see the grieving widow overwhelmed with sickness and death, and yet still having faith in Christ—Oh, what great honor these things reflect on the Good News, the Gospel of Jesus Christ!

God's grace is demonstrated—and even *magnified*—in the poverty and trials of believers. Saints summon up courage and strength throughout every discouragement, believing that all things work together for their good,[1] and that out of these things that may seem evil, a real blessing will ultimately spring up—that their God will either work a deliverance for them

---

[1] Romans 8:28.

quickly, or otherwise will most definitely support them in the trouble, for as long as He is pleased to keep them in it. This patience of the saints proves the power of divine grace.

I am thinking of a lighthouse by the edge of the sea—if it is a calm night, I will not be able to tell whether the building is strong and secure. Instead, a great storm must rage against it, and then I will know whether it will be able to stand. So it is with the Holy Spirit's work: if it were not often surrounded with stormy seas, we would not know that it was true and strong; if the winds did not blow against it, we wouldn't know how firm and secure it was. The master-works of God are those men and women who stand in the midst of difficulties, remaining steadfast and unmovable—

"Calm mid the bewildering cry,

Confident of victory."

Whoever wants to glorify God must expect to meet with many trials in life. No one can really shine brightly before the Lord unless they pass through many conflicts. If then, you are walking on a troubled path, rejoice in it, because you will be better able to prove how completely sufficient God's grace is. And as for the possibility of Him failing you—never dream of it, hate the thought!—the God who has carried you through until now, should be trusted till He calls you home to heaven.

Day 24

It is better to trust in the Lord, than to put confidence in men.

℘ Psalm 118:8 ℘

No doubt you, Dear Reader, have been tempted at times to rely upon the things which are seen, instead of resting alone upon the invisible God. Christians often look to human means for help and counsel, and disregard the noble simplicity of their reliance upon God. Is today's message being read by a child of God who is anxious and worried about the passing, temporal matters of this brief life? Then let's talk about this for a while: You trust in Jesus, and only in Jesus, for your salvation, right? Then why are you troubled?

"Because of my great burden," you might say.

But isn't it written, "Cast your burden upon the Lord"?[1] "Don't worry about anything; instead, pray about everything, telling God what you need."[2] Aren't you able to trust God with earthly matters, the temporary needs of this life?

"Ah! I wish I could," you say.

But if you cannot trust God in earthly things, how dare you trust Him for spiritual things? It doesn't make sense for

[1] Psalm 55:22; 1 Peter 5:7.
[2] Philippians 4:6.

you to trust Him for your soul's eternal redemption, and then not rely upon Him for mercy in smaller things? Isn't God enough for your needs, or is His sovereignty and control over everything still too narrow for your desires? Do you want another set of eyes, when the eyes of God Himself see every secret thing?[3] Is His heart about to give out? Is His arm tired? If so, seek another god; but if you truly believe that God is infinite, omnipotent (all-powerful), faithful, true, and all-wise, why would you travel far and wide, looking for something or someone else to put your confidence in? Why do you scour the earth to find another foundation to build upon, when your God is strong enough to bear all the weight that you could ever place on Him? Christian, just as you wouldn't mix wine with water, so also do not mix your gold of faith with the rubbish of human confidence. Wait only upon God, and let your hopeful expectation be only in Him. Don't crave after Jonah's *gourd*, that leafy plant that grew up and sheltered him from the sun, but then withered and died.[4] Instead, rest in Jonah's *God*—let fools trust in the sandy foundations[5] of human deliverance; but you, like one who sees a storm coming, build for yourself a lasting home upon the Rock of Ages.

---

[3] See Ecclesiastes 12:14 and 1 Corinthians 4:5.
[4] Jonah 4:6-11.
[5] Matthew 7:24-27.

Day 25

We must through much tribulation enter into the kingdom of God.

🐾 Acts 14:22 🐾

God's people have their trials. It was never designed by God, when He chose His people, that they should be an untested people. They were chosen in the furnace of affliction; they were never chosen to live in worldly peace and earthly joy. Freedom from sickness and the pain of this mortal life was never promised to them. No, when their Lord drew up the plans for their lives, He included discipline and correction among the things that they would inevitably receive. Trials are a part of our lot in this life; they were predestined for those of us who follow in Christ's legacy. Just as surely as the stars were created by his hands, and the orbits of the planets fixed by Him, so surely are our trials set out for us: He has chosen and ordained their season and their place, their intensity and the effect they will have upon us.

Good men and women must never expect to escape troubles; if they do, they will be disappointed, because no great Christian before them has ever been without trials and tests. For example, think about the patience of Job; or remember Abraham, for he had his trials, and by keeping his faith through them, he became the "Father of the faithful."[1] Or, stop and consider the life stories of all the patriarchs, prophets, apostles, and martyrs, and you will realize that none of those whom God used for great purposes were not first made to pass through the fire of affliction and trouble. Yes, it was ordained before the beginning of time that every "vessel of mercy"—that is, every believer, being like a cup overflowing with God's lovingkindness—should be engraved with the cross of trouble as the royal mark, marking him or her as one of the King's own special treasures.

But although trials and tribulations are the path of God's children, they have the comfort of knowing that their Master has travelled this path before them[2]; they have His presence and sympathy to cheer them, His grace to support them,[3] and His example to teach them how to endure; and when they finally reach the Kingdom of Heaven, the overwhelming joy of being there will more than make up for the trials that they had to pass through to get there.[4]

---

[1] Romans 4:11, 16.
[2] See, for example, Isaiah 53:3-4.
[3] See Hebrews 13:5-6, John 16:33.
[4] See 1 Peter 1:6-9.

Day 26

She called his name Ben-oni (son of sorrow), but his father called him Benjamin (son of my right hand).

℘ Genesis 35:18 ℘

In every difficult situation there is a bright side, as well as a dark side. Rachel was overwhelmed with the sorrow of her own tragic labor and impending death; but Jacob, even though he was weeping over the mother's loss, could see the mercy of the child's birth. And for us, even though our human nature may mourn over similar disasters, it is wonderful for us to have that triumphant faith, keeping us faithful to God through it all. The fierce lion that, at first, attacked Samson later on provided sweet honey for him,[1] and so will our hardships, if we think about them in the right way—the stormy sea feeds millions with its fish; the dark forest blooms with beautiful flowers; the driving wind sweeps away the locusts that plague the land, and the biting frost loosens the soil for new growth. Dark clouds let loose with bright raindrops, and black soil grows colorful flowers. Like a vein of gold or silver found in an old mine, so also is a vein of good found in every mine of

[1] Judges 14:5-9.

evil. Sad hearts usually find a way to view their trials with the most depressing point of view possible—if there was only one swamp in the world, they would soon be up to their necks in it, and if there was only one lion in the desert, they would hear it roar.

In all of us there is at least a hint of this terrible foolishness, and we are sometimes tempted, like Jacob, to cry, "All these things are against me."[2] But faith's way of walking is to place all of our worries and burdens upon the Lord, and then to expectantly hope for good results from the worst calamities. Like Gideon's men, faith does not get upset over the broken pottery, but instead rejoices that the torch is no longer hidden underneath, and can now blaze brightly.[3] Out of the rough oyster-shell of difficulty, true faith gathers the rare pearl of honor, and from the deep ocean-caves of distress, faith brings up the priceless coral of experience. When the waters of prosperity dry up, faith finds treasures hidden in the sands; and when the sun of delight goes down, faith turns her telescope of hope to the starry promises of heaven. When death itself appears, faith points to the light of resurrection beyond the grave, and in doing so makes our dying *Benoni* to be our strong, living *Benjamin*.

---

[2] Genesis 42:36.
[3] Judges 7:16-22.

In my prosperity I said I will never be moved.

ॐ Psalm 30:6 ॐ

The nation of Moab was like a fine wine that was allowed to settle over time; it was not emptied from one jug to another.[1] Like Moab, let a man have great wealth; let his ships continually bring home rich freight; let the winds and waves act like the man's servants to take his goods far and wide across the mighty ocean; let his lands provide abundant food, and the weather be a great help to his crops; let him always have uninterrupted success; let him stand out among his peers as a successful businessman; let him enjoy continued health; allow him to march through the world with nerves of steel and a brilliant mind, and live happily; give him a resilient spirit; let him have a song perpetually on his lips; let his eye be constantly sparkling with joy—and the natural consequence of such an easy state to any man or woman, even the best Christian who ever lived, will be *presumption*—that attitude of self-sufficiency that made even David say, "I will never be moved." And we are not as good as David, who was a man

---

[1] Jeremiah 48:11.

after God's own heart,[2] nor even half so good.

Brothers and Sisters, beware of the smooth, easy places along life's road, if you are walking them right now; or if the way is rough, thank God for it. If God were to always rock us gently in the cradle of prosperity; if we were always coddled like a baby, bouncing happily on the knees of fortune; if we didn't have some stain or blemish on this beautiful life we've envisioned for ourselves; if there weren't a few clouds in the sky; if we didn't drink some bitter drops in the wine of this life, we would definitely become intoxicated with pleasure. We would imagine we stand on our own strength in this world; and yes, we would be standing, but it would be upon a dangerous cliff, or like the man asleep high upon the mast of a ship,[3] and each moment our lives are in great danger.

We bless God, then, for our hardships; we thank Him for the unexpected changes in our lives; we give glory to His name for losses of property; for we know that if He hadn't chastened and disciplined us like this, we would have become too secure in ourselves. Yes, continued worldly prosperity is itself a fiery trial.

> *"Afflictions, though they seem severe,*
> *In mercy often are sent."*

---

[2] 1 Samuel 13:14; 16:7, 12, 13; and Acts 13:22.
[3] Proverbs 23:34.

Day 28

Man . . . is of few days, and full of trouble.

‰ Job 14:1 …

It may be of great help to us, before the day is over, to spend some time dwelling on this melancholy verse, for it may lead us to let go of some of the earthly things that we hold onto so desperately. True—there is nothing very pleasant in the realization that we are not beyond the arrows of adversity, but it may humble us and prevent our boasting like David, when he said: "I will never be moved … my mountain stands firm."[1] It may keep us from taking too deep a root in this soil, from which we are so soon to be transplanted into the heavenly garden. Let's think about this frail life that we live on earth for only a short time through God's mercies—if we would remember that all the trees of earth are marked for the woodman's axe, we would not be so eager to build our nests in them. And of course we should love life, and one another, but we should love with the love which expects death, and which plans upon separations. Our dear family members are

---

[1] Psalm 30:6.

only loaned to us temporarily, and the hour when we must return them to the lender's hand may be at the door even right now.

The same is certainly true of our worldly possessions. Don't wealth and riches just seem to grow wings and fly away? And our own health is equally uncertain and precarious— being like frail flowers of the field, we must not plan upon blooming forever. There is a time appointed for weakness and sickness, when we will have to glorify God by suffering, and not by being active and hard-working. In truth, there is no single point in life in which we can hope to escape from the sharp arrows of affliction; out of our few days on earth there is not a single one that is secure from sorrow. The life of a man or woman is much like a keg full of bitter wine; if you are seeking joy in it, you would be better off searching for honey in an ocean of salt water. Beloved Reader, don't become attached to the things of earth—don't set your affections upon them. Instead, seek those things which are above,[2] for here the moth devours, and the thief breaks in and steals,[3] but there in heaven the joy never ends—it is eternal.

The path of trouble is the way home.[4] Lord, make this thought to be a comfort to many weary souls today.

---

[2] Colossians 3:1-4.
[3] Matthew 6:19-20.
[4] See Romans 5:3-5.

Day 29

You are my hope in the day of evil.

❧ Jeremiah 17:17 ☙

The path of the Christian is not always bright with sunshine—they have their seasons of darkness and of storm. True, it is written in God's Word, "Her ways are ways of pleasantness, and all her paths are peace."[1] And it's also very true that the purpose of religion—the true religion of the Living God—is to give a person happiness below (here on earth), as well as great joy above (in heaven); but we know from experience that, even though the way of a just and righteous person is like "the light of dawn, that shines more and more until the perfect day,"[2] yet sometimes it feels like that light is eclipsed. Sometimes clouds cover the believer's sun, and they walk in darkness and don't see the light. There are many who have rejoiced in the presence of God for a season; they have basked in the sunshine in the earlier stages of their Christian life; they have walked along the "green pastures," beside the "still waters,"[3] but then all of a sudden they find that the glorious sky is now clouded; instead of living in the

---

[1] Proverbs 3:17.
[2] Proverbs 4:18.
[3] Psalm 23:2.

bountiful Land of Goshen,[4] they have to stumble through the sandy desert; in the place of sweet water to drink, they find dirty streams, bitter to their taste, and they say, "Surely, if I were a child of God, this would not happen." *But please do not say this, you who are walking in darkness!*—the best of God's saints must drink these bitter waters; the dearest of his children must bear the cross.[5] No Christian has ever enjoyed never-ending prosperity; no believer can always keep his harp from the willows.[6] Maybe the Lord at first laid out for you a smooth, sunny path, with no storm clouds overhead, because you were a weak and timid Christian. You were like a little lamb, unsteady and trembling after being sheared for the first time, and so He softened the wind for you, to keep you warm and help you along your way. But now that you are stronger in your spiritual life, you must enter into a harder and rougher experience as one of God's full-grown children. We need strong winds and driving storms to exercise our faith, to break off the rotten branches of pride, of that feeling that we can depend upon ourselves; and instead to root us more firmly in Christ. So remember, a day that just seems to be so difficult to bear, will ultimately show us the importance, the pricelessness, of our glorious hope in Christ.

---

[4] See Genesis 45. This is the good land in Egypt where Joseph moved his family, so that they would survive the seven-year famine that was happening at that time.

[5] Luke 9:23.

[6] Psalm 137:2-4. This is a reference to the captive Israelites, who could no longer bring themselves to play songs of joy on their harps after they'd been conquered and carried away to Babylon, so they hung them on willow trees.

Day 30

Are you able to hold back the stars of the Pleiades, or loosen the belt of Orion?[1]

℘ Job 38:31 ℭ

If we are ever tempted to boast or brag about our abilities, the magnificence of nature may soon show us how puny we are. We cannot move even the smallest of all the twinkling stars, or stop even so much as a single beam of morning sunshine. We human beings may speak of power, but the vastness of the skies, of the heavens above, seem to laugh at us in return. When the Pleiades[1] shine forth with the joy of spring, we can't hold back their beauty; and when Orion[1] reigns high in winter's cold darkness at year's end, we are completely unable to take its icy band of stars from the sky. The seasons revolve according to God's command, and the entire human race cannot make even the slightest change in their arrival and departure. Lord, we human beings are so incredibly small and pathetic![2]

And so also in the spiritual world, just like in the natural world, mankind's power is limited in every way. When the

---

[1] The Pleiades and Orion are two well-known star formations in the night sky, both in Biblical times and today.
[2] See, for example, Psalm 8:4: "What is man, that thou art mindful of him?"

Holy Spirit brings His delight and joy to a person's soul, no one can disturb it; all the evil schemes and hatred of men are unable to stop the warm, enlivening power of the Comforter. When He determines to visit a church and revive it, even the most hardened enemies of God cannot resist the good work—they may ridicule or mock it, but they cannot restrain it at all, just like they cannot push back the springtime, when the Pleiades rule the hour—it is God's will, and so it must be. On the other hand, if the Lord, in his sovereign plan, or to bring about justice, binds up a person so that their soul is in bondage, who is able to set them free? God alone can remove the winter of spiritual death from a person, or an entire nation. He, and no one else, loosens the belt of Orion, freeing a person from spiritual bondage, darkness, and death.

What a blessing it is that God can do these things. Oh, that He would perform this wonder today—"Lord, end my winter, and let my spring begin. No matter how hard I try, I simply can't raise my soul out of death, darkness, and despair, but all things are possible with You. I suffer much from sin and temptation—these are my terrible winter. I need your heavenly power, the brilliant shining of your love, the beaming sunrise of your grace, the light of your countenance—these are like springtime to me. Lord, please work wonders in me, and for me. Amen."

Day 31

Father, I desire that they also, whom You have given Me, be with Me where I am.

§ John 17:24 ⁂

Oh Death!, why do you take away the sheltering tree, beneath whose spreading branches the weary are able to stop and rest? Why do you snatch away the excellent of the earth, the ones who delight us so much? If you must use your axe, then use it upon the trees which give no fruit—maybe people would thank you then. But why will you chop down the magnificent cedars of Lebanon?[1] Oh, death, put your axe away, and spare the righteous…

But no, it must not be—death strikes the best of our friends—the most generous, the most prayerful, the most holy, and the most devoted all must die. And why? It is because of Jesus' prevailing prayer—"Father, I desire that they also, whom You have given Me, be with Me where I am." It is that prayer that bears them on eagle's wings to heaven.[2]

---

[1] Psalm 104:16.
[2] See Exodus 19:4 and Deuteronomy 32:11-12.

Every time a believer flies from this earth to paradise, it is an answer to Christ's prayer. A wise old Christian once said, "Many times Jesus and His people pull against one another in prayer. You kneel in prayer and say 'Father, I desire that my loved one stay with me where I am'; but Christ says, 'Father, I desire that they also, whom You have given Me, be with Me *where I am.*' And in doing so, the praying Christian is asking for the opposite of his Lord." The soul cannot be in both places—that person whom you love so much cannot be both with Christ in Heaven, and with you on the earth at the same time. Now, which prayer will win the day? If you had your choice, if the King should step from His throne, and say, "Here are two petitioners, praying in opposition to one another, which will be answered?" Oh! I am sure, even though you would be in agony, you would jump from your feet, and say, "Jesus, not my will, but yours be done." You would give up your prayer for your loved one's life, if you could realize the thoughts of Christ, praying in the opposite direction: "Father, I desire that they also, whom You have given Me, be with Me where I am."

Lord, You shall have them. By faith we let them go.

Day 32

Even though He was a Son, yet He learned obedience by the things which He suffered.

❦ Hebrews 5:8 ❧

We are told that the Captain of our salvation was made perfect through suffering[1]; therefore, we who are sinful, and who are far from being perfect, must not question God if we are also called to pass through suffering too. Will the head[2] be crowned with thorns, while the other parts of the body get to be gently rocked in a cradle of ease? Should Christ pass through seas of His own blood to win the crown, while we get to walk comfortably to heaven in silver slippers?—No, our Master's experience teaches us that suffering is necessary, and that the true-born child of God should not, must not, escape it if such a thing were possible. But there is one very comforting thought in the fact of Christ's "being made perfect through suffering"—it is that He can have complete sympathy with us, for He is "not a high priest who cannot be touched

---

[1] Hebrews 2:10.
[2] That is, Christ, the head of the church.

with the feeling of our suffering."[3] Quite the opposite—He is touched by our suffering, and it is in this sympathy of Christ that we find a power to sustain us. One of the early martyrs said, "I can bear it all, for Jesus suffered, and He suffers in me now; He sympathizes with me, and this makes me strong." Dear Believer, always hold onto this thought in times of pain. Let the thought of Jesus strengthen you as you follow in His steps. Find a sweet support in His sympathy; and further remember this—to suffer is an honorable thing, but to suffer for Christ is glory. The apostles rejoiced that they were considered worthy to do this.[4] And just as far as the Lord is gracious to us in letting us suffer for Christ—to suffer *with* Christ[5]—this is how far He honors us. The jewels of a Christian are his or her sufferings or afflictions. A Christian's troubles, sorrows, and griefs are the royal marks of God's anointing. So we should not avoid being honored. We should not run away from being exalted. Griefs exalt us, and troubles lift us up. "If we suffer, we will also reign with Him."[6]

---

[3] Hebrews 4:15.
[4] Acts 5:40-42.
[5] 1 Peter 4:12-14.
[6] 2 Timothy 2:12.

Day 33

For He has made Him to be sin for us, who knew no sin; that we might be made the righteousness of God in Him.

൩ 2 Corinthians 5:21 ൭

Dear mourning Christian!—Why are you weeping? Are you sorrowful over your own sinfulness, over your own corruptions? Look to your perfect Lord, and remember, you are complete in Him; you are in God's sight as perfect as if you had never sinned… no, actually even more than that—the Lord our Righteousness has put a divine robe upon you, so that you have more than the righteousness of mankind—you have the righteousness of God. Oh, you who are mourning because of your inborn sin and depravity, remember—none of your sins can condemn you. As a true Christian, you are learning to hate sin; but you must also learn, must also *know*, that sin is not yours—it was laid upon Christ's head. Your position of approval before God is not within yourself—it is in Christ; your acceptance is not in yourself, but in your Lord. You are as much accepted by God today, with all your sinfulness, as you will be when you stand before His throne someday, free from all corruption.

Oh, I beg of you, take hold of this precious thought—*perfection in Christ!* For you are "complete in Him."[1] With your Savior's garment on, you are as holy as the Holy one. "Who is it that could possibly condemn us? [No one!] It is Christ who died, and yes, who is risen again, who is even at the right hand of God, who also makes intercession for us."[2] Dear Christian, let your heart rejoice, for you are "accepted in the beloved"[3]— what do you have to be afraid of? Let your face always wear a smile; live near your Master; live in the suburbs of the Celestial City[4]; for soon, when your time has come, you will rise up to be with Jesus where He sits, and reign at His right hand; and it's all because the divine Lord "was made to be sin for us, who knew no sin; that we might be made the righteousness of God in Him."[5]

---

[1] Colossians 2:10.
[2] Romans 8:33-34.
[3] Ephesians 1:6.
[4] The Celestial City refers to heaven, being the ultimate goal of the main character's journey in John Bunyan's famous allegory of the Christian life, *Pilgrim's Progress*.
[5] 2 Corinthians 5:21.

Day 34

On Him they laid the cross, so that He might bear it after Jesus.

ဆ Luke 23:26 **ଔ**

When we imagine Simon of Cyrene carrying Jesus' cross,[1] we see a picture of the work of the Church throughout all generations—she is the cross-bearer after Jesus. You should realize then, Dear Christian, that Jesus did not suffer in order to prevent you from suffering. He bore a cross, not so that you may escape it, but so that you may *endure* it. Christ saves you from sin, but not from sorrow in this life. Take this reality to heart, and expect to suffer in this life.

But let us comfort ourselves with this thought—that in our case, as in Simon's, it is not *our* cross, but *Christ's* cross which we carry. When you are mistreated for your godliness; when you go through trials because of your faith, with people cruelly mocking you, then remember: It is not your cross, it is

---

[1] See also Matthew 27:32.

Christ's cross; and how delightful is it to carry the cross of our Lord Jesus!

You carry the cross after Him. You are in blessed company; your path is marked with the footprints of your Lord. The mark of His blood-red shoulder is upon that heavy burden. It is His cross, and He goes before you as a shepherd goes before his sheep. Take up your cross daily, and follow Him.[2]

Do not forget, also, that you bear this cross in partnership. Some experts believe that Simon of Cyrene only carried one end of the cross, and not the whole of it—that is very possible—Christ may have carried the heavier part, against the crossbeam, and Simon may have only held up the lighter end. Certainly it is this way with you—you only carry the lighter end of the cross, as Christ already bore the heavier end.

And remember, even though Simon had to carry the cross for a very short time, it gave him eternal honor. And in the same way, the cross we carry lasts only for a little while at most, and then we will receive the crown, the glory. Therefore, surely we should love the cross, and instead of trying to avoid it, we should consider it to be very dear to us, because it works out for us "a far more exceeding and eternal weight of glory."[3]

---

[2] Luke 9:23.
[3] 2 Corinthians 4:17.

Day 35

I will fear no evil: for You are with me.

ജ Psalm 23:4 ങ

Think of how amazing it is!—How the Holy Spirit can make a Christian so independent and free from his or her outward circumstances. What a bright light is able to shine within us when it is all dark around us! How firm, how happy, how calm, how peaceful we may be, when the world is shaken, and the earth itself seems to be falling apart! Even death itself, and every terrible thing that comes along with it, has no power to suspend the music of a Christian's heart, but instead makes that music become more sweet, more clear, more heavenly, until the last kind act which death can do is to let the earthly song blend into the heavenly chorus, the brief, passing joy of this life into the eternal bliss! Let's have confidence, then, in the blessed Spirit's power to comfort us.

Dear Reader, are you anticipating money problems in the future? Don't be afraid!—even in your need, the Holy Spirit can give you a greater feeling of satisfaction, of true wealth—much more than the rich of this world have in their abundance. You have no idea what joys may be stored up for you in the little cottage of your life, around which God's grace will plant the roses of contentment.

Are you aware of your body failing, growing weaker or sicker as time goes on? Do you expect to suffer long nights of suffering and languishing, and even longer days of pain? Oh, don't be sad! That bed that you lie in may become a throne to you. You don't realize how every ache and pain that shoots through your body could be like a refining fire to cleanse your impurities, to consume your dross,[1] or like a beam of glory to light up the secret, hidden parts of your soul.

Are your eyes losing vision, growing dim?—Jesus will be your light. Do your ears fail you, not hearing so well anymore?—Jesus' name will be your soul's best music, and His presence in your life will be your dear delight. Socrates used to say, "Philosophers can be happy without music"; and Christians can be even happier than philosophers when all outward causes of rejoicing, all external pleasures, are withdrawn. In you, my God, my heart will triumph, no matter what ill and evil things happen around me! Through your power, Oh blessed Holy Spirit, my heart will be extremely glad, even though everything should fail me here below, on Earth.

---

[1] Pastor Spurgeon is drawing a comparison here to the refining, or purifying, of precious metals, like gold, heating them until the bad parts, or "dross," are separated and then taken out, leaving only the pure metal. See also 1 Peter 1:6-9 and Job 23:10.

Day 36

*For there stood by me this night
the angel of God.*

ℰ Acts 27:23 ℭ

Raging, stormy seas, and long darkness, combined with an immediate risk of shipwreck, had destroyed the morale of the crew, all of them sad and distressed.[1] But one man alone among them remained perfectly calm, and by his words the rest were reassured. Paul was the only man who had enough heart to say, "Sirs, be of good cheer." There were veteran Roman soldiers on board, and brave old sailors, and yet their poor Jewish prisoner had more bravery than them all. He had a secret Friend who kept his courage up. The Lord Jesus sent a heavenly messenger to whisper words of consolation and comfort in the ear of His faithful servant; and so Paul's appearance and encouragement was excellent to the other men—he spoke in the voice of a man completely at ease.

If we fear the Lord,[2] we may look for God to intervene on our behalf, at just the right time, even when our situation is at its worst. Angels are not kept away from us by storms, or

---

[1] Pastor Spurgeon is referring to Paul's voyage as a prisoner to Rome, and the shipwreck that happened on the way. See Act 27:9-44 for the full account.
[2] See, for example, Proverbs 9:10. In this case, the word "fear" means a holy sense of awe, respect, and reverence for Almighty God.

hindered by darkness. Seraphs[3] don't find it at all humiliating to visit even the poorest members of the heavenly family. Even though visits from angels may be few and far between at ordinary times, they may be frequent in our nights of trouble, tempest and tossing. Our friends here on earth may drop away from us when we are under pressure, but God has power and authority to send the inhabitants of the angelic world to our aid, right when we need them—and empowered by words of love and encouragement, brought to us from His throne by the way of Jacob's ladder,[4] we will have the strength to perform the work that God sets before us.

Dear Reader, is this an hour of distress for you? If so, then ask for supernatural help. Jesus is the "angel"[5] of the covenant, and if you earnestly seek His presence, you will not be denied. And then, like Paul, when the anchors would no longer hold, and their ship was almost upon the rocks, you'll remember that you've had the angel of God standing by you in a night of storm.

> *"O angel of my God, be near,*
> *Amid the darkness hush my fear;*
> *Loud roars the wild tempestuous sea,*
> *your presence, Lord, will comfort me."*

---

[3] Seraphim are a particular type of angel mentioned in the Bible; see Isaiah 6.

[4] Genesis 28:10-19.

[5] In this case, Pastor Spurgeon is referring to Jesus as an angel because the Greek word actually means "messenger." See also Malachi 3:1, which is likely a reference to Jesus as the "Messenger" (angel) of the covenant.

*Say to the righteous,
that it will be well with them.*

so Isaiah 3:10 cs

It is well with the righteous ALWAYS. If the Bible verse had said, "Say to the righteous, that it is well with them *in their prosperity*," then we would be thankful to God for protecting us when things are going well, because prosperity can actually be a time of danger, leading us into sin if we are not careful. Or, if it had been written, "It is well with them when they are being mistreated or oppressed," then we would be thankful for such a protecting and sustaining promise, because oppression is so hard to bear. But because *no time* is mentioned in the verse, this means that *all time* is included. God's "wills" must be understood always in their largest sense, as great as you can imagine—from the beginning of the year to the end of the year, from the first gathering of evening shadows until the morning-star shines, in all conditions and under all circumstances, it will be well with the righteous. It is so well with him or her that we couldn't possibly imagine it to be better, for they are well fed: they feed upon the flesh and blood of Jesus[6]; they are well clothed: they wear the

---

[6] See John 6:32-35, 41, 48-69.

righteousness of Jesus Christ that has now been attributed to them[7]; they are well housed: they dwell in God[8]; they are well married: their souls are knit in bonds of marriage union to Christ[9]; they are well provided for: for the Lord is their Shepherd[10]; they are altogether rich and wealthy, for Heaven is their inheritance.[11]

It is well with the righteous—well, based upon God's authority; the mouth of God Himself speaks the comforting assurance. Oh Beloved Reader, if God declares that all is well, then ten thousand devils may speak of doom and evil, and say that everything is going wrong, but we're able to knowingly laugh at them all—praise be to God for a faith that enables us to believe God when all the rest of the world contradicts Him. If you are a righteous child of God, then the Word of God says that it is *always* well with you, at all times and in every place—if you still have trouble seeing this truth, then let God's word stand up for you in the place of your own sight; yes, rely on the authority of God's Word more confidently than if your own eyes and your own feelings told you so.

Whomever God blesses is truly blessed indeed, and whatever His lips declare is the most certain and enduring truth there is.[12]

---

7 Revelation 3:5, 7:13-14. See also 2 Corinthians 5:21 and Revelation 3:5.
8 John 15:4-11; Revelation 21:3; 1 John 4:13.
9 Ephesians 5:25-27, 32; Revelation 19:6-8.
10 John 10:10-16; Psalm 23.
11 1 Peter 1:3-9; Romans 8:14-17; Ephesians 13-14, 18.
12 See Hebrews 6:17-20.

Day 38

Lift them up forever.
✍ Psalm 28:9 ✍

God's people need lifting up. They are very heavy by nature—
they have no wings; or, if they do have them, they are like the
dove spoken of in the Bible, lying low on the ground; and they
need grace from God to make them take flight on wings covered
with silver, and with feathers of yellow gold.[1] It's natural that
sparks from a fire will fly upward, [2] but the sinful souls of men
fall downward. Oh Lord, "lift them up forever!" David himself
said, "Unto you, Oh God, do I lift up my soul,"[3] and here he also
feels the need to ask God to lift up other men's and women's
souls as well as his own. So, when you ask this blessing for
yourself, don't forget to ask it for others also.

There are three ways that God's people need to be lifted
up. First, they require to be elevated in character—Lift them up,
Oh Lord; do not allow your people to be like the world's people!
The world lies low, it wallows, in service to the wicked one,[4] to
Satan; but Dear Lord, lift your people out of it![5] The world's
people are constantly chasing after silver and gold, seeking their

---

[1] Psalm 68:13.
[2] Job 5:7.
[3] Psalm 25:1.
[4] 1 John 5:19.
[5] 1 John 2:13-14.

own pleasures, and indulging in their own lusts; but, Lord, lift your people up above all this; keep them from being "muck-rakers," as John Bunyan calls the man who was always scraping after gold![6] Lord, please set their hearts upon their risen Lord and their heavenly inheritance![7]

Secondly, believers need to be lifted up and prospered in conflict. In the battle, if they seem to fall, Oh Lord, please give them the victory still.[8] If the foot of the enemy is on their neck, holding them down even for a moment, please help them to grasp the sword of the Spirit,[9] and eventually to win the battle. Lord, lift up your children's spirits in the day of conflict; don't let them sit in the dust, in sadness and mourning forever. Don't allow the adversary, the enemy, to frustrate them into despair and worry. Instead, if they have been persecuted and put down, like Hannah, let them sing of the mercy of a God who delivers them from trouble.[10]

And finally, we can also ask our Lord to lift up His people at the very end! Lift them up by taking them home, lift their bodies from the tomb, and raise their souls to your eternal kingdom in glory.[11] Amen.

---

[6] See Pilgrim's Progress; this is the man who is always seeking after worldly gain by raking (searching) through filth in search of gold.

[7] See Ephesians 2:1-10 and 4:17-24.

[8] 1 Corinthians 15:56-58.

[9] See Ephesians 6:10-20 for the Full Armor of God, including the sword of the Spirit, which is the Word of God.

[10] 1 Samuel 1:1 – 2:11.

[11] John 14:1-3; 1 Corinthians 15:20-28, 42-54; 1 Thessalonians 4:13-18.

Day 39

You will not be afraid of the terror by night.

≈ Psalm 91:5 ≈

What is this terror? It may be the cry of fire, or the noise of thieves, or the thought of something scary in the dark, or the scream of sudden sickness or death. We live in the world of death and sorrow, so we're just as likely to see these things during the nighttime hours as beneath the glare of the afternoon sun. And regardless, whatever the terror may be, the promise in this verse is that the believer "will not be afraid." Why should he be? Or, let us ask it a little closer to the heart—why should *we* be afraid?—God our Father is here, and *will be* here all through the lonely hours; He is an almighty Watcher, a sleepless Guardian, a faithful Friend.[1] Nothing can happen without His direction, for even hell itself is under His control. Darkness is not dark to him. He has promised to be a wall of fire around his people[2]—and who can break through such a barrier? People of this world, nonbelievers, may very well be afraid, for they have an angry God above them, a guilty

---

[1] John 15:13-15.
[2] Zechariah 2:5.

87

conscience within themselves, and a wide-open hell beneath them; but we who rest in Jesus are saved from all these through God's rich mercy. If we give in to foolish fear, we dishonor our Christian profession of faith, and lead others to doubt the reality of godliness. Instead, we ought to be afraid *of being afraid*; otherwise, we might grieve the Holy Spirit[3] by our foolish lack of trust.

So, then, say "good-bye" to all those dismal thoughts of doom, and those fearful moments of panic and anxiety—God has not forgotten to be gracious and loving, nor has He shut up and held back His tender mercies. It may feel like night in your soul, but there doesn't need to be any terror there, for the God of love never changes! Children of light such as yourself may walk in darkness, but that doesn't mean at all that they have been forgotten or cast aside. To the contrary—they now have a tremendous opportunity to prove the truth of their adoption as God's children, by trusting in their Heavenly Father[4]—something that hypocrites and pretenders cannot do.

> *"Though the night be dark and dreary,*
> *Darkness cannot hide from thee;*
> *Thou art he, who, never weary,*
> *Watchest where thy people be."*

---

[3] Ephesians 4:30.
[4] Romans 8:14-16.

Day 40

That through death he might destroy him

that had the power of death.

෨ Hebrews 2:14 ෫

Oh Child of God, death has lost its sting, because the devil's power over it is destroyed. So you should no longer fear dying. Ask for mercy, for grace from God the Holy Spirit, that He would give you a deep knowledge, and a firm belief in the sacrificial death of Jesus, your Redeemer, so that you may be strengthened for that final hour. If you live near to the cross of Calvary,[5] in your heart and in your mind, you'll be able to think of death with pleasure, and welcome it when it comes with intense delight. It is a sweet thing to die in the Lord; it is God's keeping of the covenant that He made with His people. Yes, it is truly a blessing from God to "fall asleep"[6] in the love and salvation of Jesus. Death is no longer a banishment from life; instead, it is like a return from exile, a going home to the

---

[5] See Luke 23:33 in the King James Bible for a description of Calvary, where Jesus was crucified. Other versions translate this as the Place of the Skull.
[6] The Bible often speaks of Christians who have died as merely "asleep." See, for example, 1 Corinthians 15:6 or 1 Thessalonians 4:15.

many mansions[7] where many of our loved ones are already living and waiting for us. The distance may seem great between those glorified saints in Heaven, and the Christians still fighting the battle here on earth, but this isn't true. In reality, we are not far from home—a brief moment will bring us there:

The sail is spread open, and the soul is launched upon the vast deepness of space—how long will be its voyage? How many gusting winds must beat upon that sail before it will pull into that peaceful harbor? How long will that soul be tossed up and down on the waves before it comes to that sea where it never storms? Listen to the answer, "Absent from the body, present with the Lord."[8] That ship we've been talking about has just departed, but it is already at its safe haven. It only had to spread its sail, and it was there. Like that ship from long ago, upon the Sea of Galilee, a storm came up and the waves and wind threatened to sink it, but Jesus said, "Peace, be still," and immediately it came to land.[9] So, don't think that there's a long, intervening period between the instant of death and the eternity of glory. When the eyes close on earth, they open in heaven. Those chariots of fire[10] that carry a person to heaven won't linger for an instant on the road. Knowing all

---

[7] John 14:2 (see KJV specifically for use of the word "mansions").
[8] 2 Corinthians 5:8.
[9] See Mark 4:36–41 and John 6:16–21.
[10] 2 Kings 2:11.

this now, Dear Child of God, what is there for you to fear in death, seeing that through the death of your Lord, its curse and sting are destroyed?[11]

And now, death is nothing more than a Jacob's ladder,[12] with its feet in the dark grave, but its top reaching up to

Everlasting Glory.

---

[11] 1 Corinthians 15:54-58.
[12] Genesis 28:10-17.

Thank You for Reading!

We hope these devotionals have been an encouragement to you these past forty days. If they've made a difference to you, please let us know by writing us at:

rpbnorthern@outlook.com

R.P.B. Northern Publishing Company is a small, independent publisher. We focus only on wholesome books. If this book made a difference to you, please consider writing a positive review online, and spread the word to your friends and family!

Notes:

Notes:

Notes: